Qalb

Poetry

Minela Hadzic

BookLeaf Publishing

India | USA | UK

Made with ❤ on the BookLeaf Publishing Platform
www.bookleafpub.in
www.bookleafpub.com

Dedication

Praise and Thanks be to my Lord.
To a place where the sun rises and the moon never
sleeps.

Preface

We all have days of hardship, Dunya , this life created to break us or make us. This set of poetry belongs solely to my heart.
Written for my journey

Acknowledgements

Thank you to all those who have been a part of writing this book.

1. Duaas

Oh My Lord Thank you
For the opportunity
For these very hands
To callout to thee.

A bridge to my Lord
Solace to my hands,
Comfort to my heart.

Since I can remember
Til' my last breath forever
Ever and ever.
A line between my Lord and I
You are my ammunition
Til' the day I die.

Heart ready to fall
Words of conviction
Sincerest call.

When I think i'm falling
You descend to the lowest Heaven
To hear my calling.

Praising you too,
Glorifying you all day
And all night through...

Dear Lord bestow your mercy,
Forgiveness on my soul
Comfort my heart
Take all control

2. Allah, You and I.

3

Guide my heart to him my Lord, wherever he may be.
If you love him and he's pleasing, bring him closer to me.

Guide my heart my dear Lord, steadfast and consistent
Make my soul firm on deen, loving and persistent.

Guide my beloved to me my Lord, bring us closer
together
So we can obey and please you from now til' forever.

Ameen.

You are my soulmate, yet you'll never know are
I feel lost without you , it's dark and you're the star

You're the missing piece in my puzzle, today
Please make yourself known and be here to stay.

You are my soulmate , there is no doubt

It's not the one you can live with, it's who you can't live
without.

I'm lost and distracted, i'm losing my sabr
You are my soulmate. It is in my qadr.

Know that I am waiting, for you to show up soon,
You can be my sun , I will be your moon.

3. Ihsan

Like the river flowing through my veins,
I embrace you.
Your beauty and your calm.
Like a raindrop I hold you close
In the middle of my palm.
I can't let go afraid i'll lose you
In the willowing breeze
If I let you fall from me
I may die so please
Lord of Heavens and the Earth
Allow me to keep it
Calmly so serene so beautiful for whats its worth
And should it fall from the skin contact it will
Be against me , on The day of all days
When I bow before you.
Should a tear fall from my eye and if I don't
Whisper ameen
The world will stare in awe of all
I've ever been and if seen with a green eye
May you grant me protection,

Eternal Loving Merciful
With nothing but affection.
Excellent is He who created me
With intricate precision
Unique and beautiful with Will and decision
So when I look in the mirror I see a heart
Full of love , beauty and compassion.
Dare I say my face is as beautiful as the heart
And there goes the ruh the akhlak piercing my eyes
A tear falls and slides down my face
Skin contact and all that's mine slowly embraced
I whisper 'ameen' and turn away
Taking with me an image I'll never forget
In awe of my Creator , the character a lot.
Hearing , Seeing and Knowing all in all
I lower my gaze but still stand so tall.
Should I leave this world
And no one else to part
Say goodbye and bow one last time.
If no one remembers me
Just as an Insan
May they see the vision in me
The excellent Ihsan.

4. Sabr

Test after test after test, devastation , grief.
Hardship after hardship feels like a thief.
Devastation.
I pray and wait for the outcomes that may come
Then I am back at square one and some.

I'm sad but awaiting my promised reward
Maybe in this life or the next and
I don't know at all.

Distance from My Rabb is not so long or far
What I await is to difficult to bear
And no matter How close or far you are
I know you're always there.

For time has served me well and I've said this before
I sometimes sit and cry
So you pour mercy into my soul , love and
I don't know why.

It's your care and love your beautiful Rahma
And the more I sit and endure
The Hardships the calamities
Of this life am sure.

5. Qalb

Purified intentions
Good deeds
Salah
Smiles
Happy moments
Sad moments
Memories
Feelings
Love
Truth of certainty
Ihsan
Akhlak
Nur
Loving people
Family
Friends
Everyone
Neverending
Gratitude
Appreciation

Patience
I endure.
Hearts
Butterflies
Leaves falling
Nature
Animals
Plants
All living things
Angels.

6. Love

Mercy and Compassion
Happiness and Joy
Peace

Serene

Tranquility and Calm
Beauty and Character
Empathy.

Fun
Hope and Trust
Faith and Belief
Complete.

Pray
Patience and Gratitude
Appreciation
Life.

7. La ilaha ilallah

Before I fall asleep for good, outside of my bed
I hope they'll let me say it and some coffee for my head
Like the echo on the
mountains
A speckle in the sand
I hope they all remember me
And...

Be my friends in the end before I close my eyes
Maybe on a friday just before sunrise
I may not get the chance to pray my 2 rakaat
Like they're the last ones of this temporary life

And should they talk about me, i know this is much is
true
I loved the Qur'an and the Qur'an loved me
Too...
It's like an honour killing ,
bleeding me to death
Hurting my soft heart

Taking my last breath
I find myself suffocating
At the slightest thought
That i loved them
And they didnt love me at all.

Like a gem or pebble thrown about the road
They might remember me shy, lowered gaze
But still standing there tall

They know my biggest rise and my darkest fears
They're in my duuas falling with my tears
Ill not surrender i'll let them have their intention
I'm tired of this life, its pretension

So yes im facing death and i hope they let me say it
Some coffee for my head, a tear a smile
For my kabur as my bed.

They might think it's over
But it's only for a while
One day on that day
They'll see me rise with a smile

What to write next,
I don't really know
But i hope they will see me

In the glitter of snow.

15

8. Asr

When the angels alternate,
Through sorrow and the pain.
Sabr and perseverance
And certainty,
I pray

In my kushoo state,
When all else is silent
I engage my heart like that abd that I am
And move forward washing of the sins
Before it begins
To cry in my heart
The nur of my soul

Then i'm in awe of my Rabb and I
As I engage with my last cries.
Alhamdulillah so grateful for my salah
And without it i'm so incomplete
I'm in awe still

And I always will be.

As I bow for my Lord and offer my sincere,
Prayer until the next meeting that is always so near
With every beat of my heart I can't escape
I love you my Lord !
I love you my Lord!

9. Subhanakallahum

I wish for a white horse with white and silver wings,
Rivers that flow full of honey and milk.
Pomegranate trees olives and figs
Olives and white roses scattered all over
Snowdrops with dewdrops and the smell of snow
Or after the rain scent that leaves me in awe.

I wish to have a home full of things i love or
Will it just be a garden of magical fun
I need some butterflies , white ones of course
And bees perhaps with honey like ones in this world
I wish for sakinah and pure joy,
a tranquil heart full of peace that i will enjoy

I wish for no sorrow and wish for no grief
I wish for so much more but im remaining brief
Laughter of those i loved in dunya and gardens looking
out
Towards the waterfalls i can't live without
Maybe some rivers in colours i have not seen

Shiny and glittering like places i've never been

I wish for silky gowns in green and white
Cushions comfy like clouds and shining bright
I wish for all the good i've not felt in this world
I like white and silver, not diamond or gold.

I wish for books in the sky and as i look up i see the
righteous
like the stars in this world except no one is jealous
I wish to feel its zeal and feel the warmest breeze
Wish everyone happiness and finally ease.

I wish for the longest day like this than i can imagine
To keep smiling all day long and love myself some more
To be free finally and spread my wings a bit like the
horse
I will call Bentley.
I will wish one more thing and that's from this world
That every righteous enters the gardens beneath which
rivers flow.

I wish for them happiness , tranquility and joy
And all that they wish too that they will enjoy.

10. Alhamdulillah

Grateful for the blessings
For my lungs I breathe with
For the lips and the tongue I speak with
Hearing
Eyesight
Heart and soul
Grateful for the way I walk
That I can, walk.
Grateful for my roof
For my children
For the laughter and the smiles
Tears and the cries.

Grateful for the blessings
Mercy
Love and care.
Guidance
Sakinah
Kushoo
His words.

Grateful for the blessings
Prayers
Duaas
Opportunity for deeds
Charity
Sunnah

The sun, the moon and the stars
The sea , the mountains ,the clouds
Butterflies, roses, wildflowers
Rivers and the pebbles
The fish and the animals

The trees and the nature
All the pretty scenes
Picturesque and serene
All that He created
Living things like
Insects yes the ants too
Spiders and ladybugs
That fly and dandelions
Alhamdulillah.

11. Autumn in winter

Like the blessed rain , the leaves fall ,the butterflies leave until spring when all blossoms with the most beautiful trees are then dressed in green. The scent of linden and honey in the air.

I'm in awe, just before dawn when eyes are sleeping and all is silenced can you hear the whispers of my heart.

The thread to my Lord from the qalb pouring, like the rain vulnerabilities, sorrow and love.

The butterflies and ladybugs have left for the season , the squirrels are burying for the winter, the season ahead.

Before the snow falls and covers the land in glistening white blankets, the quiet snow falls like the memories of my darkest moments. The cold air penetrating through the windows of my soul , I stand still for the moment and offer sincerest duas for those I love the most. My eyes trickle the hottest tears that then slide down my face covering me in sadness, releasing my heart into the surroundings and I whisper 'Ameen'.

Resigning to bed praying to God that should I die may it be upon deen, and should I live may I live upon faith. To follow my heart to the best of my ability now cleansed, sincere and certain. Certain that it is the Lord's decree,

Typing each letter and word now reminiscing the dark moments, moments of cold and sadness reminds me of what has passed. The Lord promised what is to come is better, so I await with silent patience, that's almost spent.

I feel like crying. I feel like i'm dying, like the end is near yet remind myself the end is just a start. I cannot complain though my heart yearns, peace and freedom from this world, and I need to be deserving.

I connect the puzzles and feel better for the moment waiting for the next test, to jump a hurdle, to face a dark night, a moment which sometimes lasts forever.

In the hope to wake up elsewhere and smile for the sake of Him who created me just for the purpose to worship and love Him, alone.

No one else in sight to disturb my final moment before I return my spirit to this life to wake up smell the coffee and face reality to the best of my ability, I falter and fall each day before day turns to night, hoping to close my eyes one final time and take a flight, to the next bridge- bridge to the one remembered.

12. (Star)

The day switches off and night takes over
enveloping the globe in darkness. A shade to cover the
sky that pierces through the moonlight, speckled like
midnight canvas with the most beautiful stars.
Stupendous Lord, who created the Heavens and the
Earth, sitting on the throne of the Arsh.
Waiting for a call from those fearful and obedient
seeking forgiveness and blessings, awaiting their return -
the next life.
For their names to be called at the gates and the
trumpet to be blown just before, then in fear awaken
resurrected and waiting in a row. For the scales and the
record books and reports of all they used to do.
In this world everyone has their favourite star ,
guiding through the night of dunya, nur and speckle.

13. Repentance

I raise my hands to you my Lord,
I seek protection from all evil created in this word.
Seeking help from harm and away from your wrath and
asking for forgiveness, a sincere calling. For I have
sinned, forgive me please , this is out of my control.
I can't help my feelings please remove them from my
heart, I can't sleep.
Forgive me please my Lord!

Ameen

Tawba

Astagfirullah Astagfirullah Astagfirullah wa atubu ilaihi.
I return to you in repentance.
I plead with you to take my whole being into your own
hands.

The rightful owner of my heart and soul.

Ameen

Regrets

I regret the moment I met Vahid in my life.
I loved this man, for a while
Not in my control, my heart is taken over by desire.
So I repent the moment I felt this way.
May you forgive me my Lord

Ameen

14. The ones within

Violation, stripped of my human rights,
The duration of their control invasion
Days and all the nights.
A fright that has no end or so it seems,
Can't fight them off
Wanting what i can't give
Even less to take from them,
Invaded dreams, alternate voices
Everyone taking turns to kill me
That little more inside.
Nightmares and dreams alike
Noisy, then quiet all at the same time
Power or so they think
Their magic and mine too
Mine in my heart theirs in their dirty nafs
Just won't leave me alone
Leaving me fragile
Leaving me tired, extremely tired
If only for the night i could sleep in peace
What is peace?

Drama, talks, defamation, slander
Dry banter unintended love
Lies and deceit.
Lies and deceit.
Dishonesty minus integrity
No hope, dark, no light
Scared. Afraid. Distorted images
Memories
Reminiscing, pain, it hurts.
Sensations , disturbing..
Irritation , annoying , neverending.
Negative intrusive and distant thoughts
Yet I am still here, paralysed frozen and it goes on.
They won't leave me alone,,,
Leave me alone!

15. Believe in YOUrself

Stay humble, stand tall
They cannot harm you at all.
Be honest be You no one in this world
Is truer than you.

Walk with purpose stand your ground
You're the best thing they've ever found
Know your worth , boundaries an all
Stay humble and stand tall.

Be kind in a cruel and cold world
Be the one someone turns to
Be generous, compassionate and understanding
When everyone leaves, be the last one to remain
standing

Leave a legacy of kindness, honesty integrity and
love
Carry faith, belief and trust above.
When you leave the world leave a trace

Because no one but you can ever embrace
Their love and flaws and shortcomings,

Be a light in their dark ,
Be a smile in their frown
Be there and never let them down.
Be You in the cold world
Stay humble and stand tall.

Walk the path of righteousness and always stay
patient
Be a woman of virtue and fix the crown on your
head
Never plant kisses on cheeks
And remember who planted one on your forehead.

Have self respect and move in firmness
Steadfastness and conviction
No one can replace you in this world
Remain kind with addiction.

Stay true to yourself and others
Love the ground you walk on
Worship thy Lord with submission
And love Him like He's The only one worth it.

16. Detachment

I am divorcing Dunya, like you would divorce the one you once loved. Getting away from the unnecessary, I am divorcing and detaching from dunya like my last breath for freedom. I'm cutting the cord from dunya. It's the last time it can hurt me.

From darkness of my heart to the nur of the soul I'm saying goodbye to dunya and everything in it, the boring dunya that's so beautiful but for the moment. Beautified by shaitan to attract and distract us for the whole duration here, i don't want it.

Im divorcing dunya because im in love with a man who cannot be mine and am detaching my heart and building my akhirah starting right now. This temporary dunya is a bridge not a home, having to fall and commit a sin, or two or three.

Im detaching myself from Dunya from this moment on from its problems and issues, from its worries, from its grief and sorrow, detaching from yesterday, today and tomorrow - I want my next life am sure it's true ... I'm so happy I'm leaving you, dunya.

17. Timeless

The closest friend
The book of all books
My inspiration
My motivation.
My best friend.
The Holy words
His Majesty
The Compassionate
The Merciful
The LOving
The Kind.
The more i listen
The more sakinah
The Originator
The Responder
The Oft Forgiving
His words
Weaved like a spider web
That i've never seen before

Like a painting not painted before
Like a poet no one ever heard
His Majesty
My Lord.
In awe
Amazing
Wonderful
Unique and beautiful.
The One.
The Only One
Containing the missing pieces of the puzzle
The puzzle in my heart.
The only and only

Book of all books
The Holy Qur'an.

18. Heart

Heart in my throat,
Love in the heart
Words on my tongue
You name in my soul.

I love you.

For sake of Him,
For you , for me.
I love you ,
I love you ,

With everything i am
No one compares to you
Your smile.
I love you.

I need you like the air i breathe
I can't explain or describe
Your neither here nor there

Mine nor not mine.

I love you,
Like the rain loves the earth,
Like desert loves rain
Like the butterflies and bees
Who love flowers

Like i love you from the bottom of my heart
I love you to the Arsh and back.
I need you right now
I love you.
I love you.

19. Death by Heart

Torn, hurt, pained by the words of the one I love the
most here.
I'm not in the mood for life any longer, am neither in this
life nor the next.
I have entered a dimension in between lost between two
worlds
He's making me sick with disappointment.

I feel my heart ripped out of my being.
My body paralysed ,
My mind is insane.
I guess the pen is lifted.
I fell for shaitans tricks
And if i may say
Am to blame not him.

Depressed heart, one that was full of pure love for
humanity
Is now diluted in the tears of my soul, wanting more
from him.

Whilst he watches me undisturbed untouched unmoved.
Making me hate that i love him
Please forgive me my Lord this is my last plea
Remove him, remove him from me. Ameen

20. River

Tonight, within me a river flowing,
fighting, tugging at the river bed.
Hot and cold roots are growing,
seeds of words that were unsaid.

Tonight, within me a river drying,
Drying , fading at the river bed.
Scared of fear and of dying,
in the world of the living dead.

Tonight, withing me a river running,
In my heart ripping its chains,
Letting go of all the poison,
That grew and flew through my veins.

Tonight, within me a River is dying,
under the shadow of grey skies,
Slowly, taking each my breath,
and trickling through the doors of my eyes.

Tonight, under a bridge I cry,
and send away my last tear.
I become who I once was
without doubt , without fear.

Tonight, a new me is born.
under the bridge of new streams.
my soul and heart are no longer torn
I have new hopes , I have new dreams.

In sha Allah!

21. Smile

Happy days are rare indeed,
And sometimes seem so far,
But let me remind you all,
Just how wonderful you ARE.

You wake-up each morning,
And get on with your day,
No matter how hard times are
You believe and pray.

When the world goes cold,
Life is hard to bare,
Smile and keep smiling
And you'll always find me there.

Thank God for each day,
For everything is His,
And words alone can hardly say,
How beautiful life is.

So when you're feeling low,
Smile and count to five,
Take a deep, deep, breath
And remember you're alive.

You can't put a value on life,
Like you can on things,
And if we didn't have those we love,
Imagine what we'd miss.

So wake up each morning,
Smile and say,
I'm so lucky to be alive,
What a beautiful day.

Live your life full of love
For everyone to see,
it's not about what you're looking at,
It's about how you see.

www.ingramcontent.com/pod-product-compliance
Lightning Source LLC
La Vergne TN
LVHW050945200726
843508LV00011B/2445